The Winner

Written by Amy Algie

Illustrated by Ian Forss

"What's up, Steve? You seem a bit quiet this morning," said Dad.
"Mike's coming today.
I thought you'd be excited.
You always have fun together."

Steve looked up from his breakfast.
"I'm all right, Dad," he said.

3

Steve liked his cousin, Mike.
They did have fun together.
But Mike always wanted
to beat Steve. He always wanted
to play games that he could win.
Mike would do *anything* to win.

"There's Mike now," said Dad.

Steve looked outside. "Hi, Mike," he called. "It's good to see you."

Mike walked along the path holding a baseball bat in one hand and bouncing a basketball with his other hand.

"Hi, Steve," he shouted. "Come on out and have some fun."

Steve sighed and walked outside.

Mike bounced the ball.
"Come and get it," he called.

Steve tried to get the ball,
but whenever he got near it,
Mike jumped into the air
and shot it through the hoop.

"Now you try," said Mike,
and he gave the ball to Steve.

Steve aimed for the hoop, but the
ball hit the rim and bounced into
Mike's waiting hands.

9

"Let's pitch a few balls," said Mike.

Steve felt like crying. Mike always pitched the ball so hard that he didn't have a hope of hitting it.

Steve pitched a good ball, and Mike whacked it straight back at him. He laughed when Steve ducked out of the way.

Dad came to join in.
"You field, Steve," he said.
"I'll pitch a few balls to Mike."

Dad pitched the ball and Mike whacked it high into the air.

"Catch it, Steve," called Dad,
but Steve missed, and Mike
laughed again.

"Cheer up, Steve," whispered Dad
when they went inside for lunch.
Then he said to both the boys,
"I have an idea for this afternoon.
Let's play mini golf."

"I've never played mini golf,"
said Mike doubtfully.

"You'll like it," said Dad as he
grinned at Steve.

Dad handed the boys their clubs.
Mike waved his club in the air.
"This looks easy," he said.
"I bet I can beat you, Steve."

Mike walked up to his ball and
whacked it hard. The ball bounced
off the track into some bushes.
"That's out of bounds," said Dad.
"That's two points. You must
start again."

Steve hit the ball carefully.
It rolled under the bridge
and stopped right by the hole.

"Nice shot, Steve," said Dad.
Steve grinned proudly.

Mike hit his ball again. It rolled
to the bridge and stopped.
"That's three shots," said Dad.

Steve tapped his ball in for two.
Dad hit his in for three.
Mike took two more shots before
he got his ball into the hole.

"Nice going, Steve," said Dad.
"You won that hole."

At the next hole, Steve took
three shots, Dad took four,
and Mike took six.

"This isn't as easy as it looks,"
said Mike.

19

They hit the balls through castles.

They hit the balls over bridges.

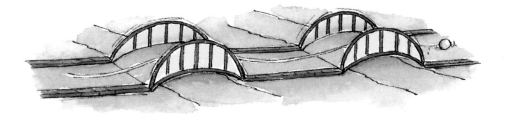

They hit the balls around water.

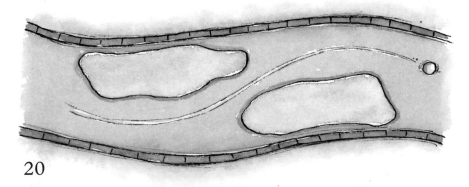

After each hole, they wrote down their scores.

"You're really good at this, Steve," said Mike.

"Thanks, Mike," said Steve. "I've played a few games with Dad."

At the end of the game, Dad added up the scores. Mike got eighty-eight. Dad got seventy-two and Steve got sixty-one.

"Well done, Steve," Dad said with a big smile. "You're the winner!"

Mike threw his ball at Steve. "Catch!" he shouted. Steve missed.

"Got you!" laughed Mike. "Can we play mini golf tomorrow, Uncle John? It's fun."

START